# Family Walks
# in Suffolk

## C. J. Francis

HIGH INTEREST · LOW MILEAGE

Scarthin Books of Cromford
Derbyshire
1993

**Family Walks in Suffolk**

*General Editor*: Norman Taylor

**The Country Code**

Enjoy the countryside and respect its life and work
Guard against all risk of fire
Fasten all gates
Keep your dogs under close control
Keep to public paths across farmland
Use gates and stiles to cross fences, hedges and walls
Leave livestock, crops and machinery alone
Take your litter home
Help to keep all water clean
Protect wildlife, plants and trees
Take special care on country roads
Make no unnecessary noise

**Walking the routes in this book**

All the routes in this book have been walked, in most cases, several times prior to publication and we have taken great care to ensure that they are on rights of way. However, changes occur all the time in the landscape; should you meet any obstructions, please let us know. Serious obstructions can be brought to the attention of the local branch of the Ramblers Association and the Rights of Way section of the County Council.

Published by Scarthin Books of Cromford, Derbyshire 1993

Printed in Great Britain at The Alden Press, Oxford

ISBN 0907758 649

*Illustrations*: Stuart Ling
*Cover illustration*: Andrew Ravenwood. Framlingham Castle (Route 2)

Bridleway, Trimley St Mary (route 5)

**Dedication**

To my wife, Janet, who accompanied me on most of the walks

**Acknowledgements**

Thanks to Stuart Ling for his pen and ink drawings

**About the Author**

C. J. Francis was born and bred in Suffolk and is a civil servant by profession. His hobbies of bird watching and rambling have taken him on and off the beaten track around the county. This is his first book.

# Contents

# Map of the Area

# Introduction

Suffolk offers a wide variety of delights to discover and enjoy. The routes in this book are based on a fraction of the 3,000-odd miles of public footpath and rights of way to be found in the county. Save for the occasional gentle climb or descent, most of the walking is on the level along a well-defined network of paths, tracks and bridleways. There are opportunities to explore undulating parkland, stroll through rolling countryside and walk the towpaths of slow moving rivers. Most of the waymarked routes can be walked any time during the year. The local scene on a warm summer's evening will of course differ from that encountered under a clear blue sky with a light sprinkling of frost.

For example, on the clifftop at Dunwich, nowadays no more than a small village, you can gaze out to sea and imagine how this once ancient capital of East Anglia looked before being swallowed up over the centuries by the encroaching tide. A local legend has it that if you listen carefully you can hear a muffled peal of bells from churches buried beneath the waves.

Inland at Flatford there is the opportunity to follow in the footsteps of the landscape artist, John Constable. The countryside may have changed since Constable's day, but it's still possible to visit sites where the artist painted well-known scenes such as the *Hay Wain*.

The walk at Framlingham is dominated by the massive castle; climb the spiral staircase where boisterous youngsters can shout: 'I'm the King of the Castle.' The climb is also worthwhile for a commanding view of the surrounding countryside.

Other routes take you along open heathland once frequented by Neolithic man; grand churches and pretty villages founded on wealth from the medieval cloth trade beckon the explorer. Many of the walks pass through meadows and woodland and during the springtime especially you are likely to hear the sound of birdsong and find the ground carpeted with wild flowers such as primroses, cowslips and bluebells.

## Interest

The walks have been written with the family very much in mind. Hopefully you will find each walk informative and entertaining rather than a dull trudge around the countryside. Obviously with younger children distance will be an important factor to consider. Unless their interest is maintained boredom will start to creep in. Some walks include activities such as the chance to indulge in a game of poohsticks, feed and watch ducks, fly a kite and play ball. Older children (as well as adults) might find binoculars useful as well as pocket reference books containing details of birds, trees and plants etc.

## Weather and Clothing

In Suffolk there is a saying that a cold easterly wind is lazy – it goes through you rather than around you. The message, therefore, is to wrap up well. Some walks offer little protection from the elements. With no quick return to the car-park, being caught in an isolated spot without appropriate clothing is no joke. One remedy is to keep an eye on local weather conditions. If the outlook remains uncertain a useful tip is to phone the local weatherline (0603 66077) and listen to the latest forecast.

## Transport to the Area

For the purposes of this book it's assumed that most families will have access to a car and therefore will have little difficulty in reaching individual starting points. Public transport in some rural parts of the county is almost non-existent. However, where routes can reasonably be reached by bus or train, relevant transport operators have been listed accordingly.

## Refreshments

Places for refreshments have been listed at selected points on each walk. In the main, names of public houses offering traditional fare have been given. Most welcome children and often provide picnic tables as well as a mini play area. To cater for other tastes, where possible, tearooms and cafes have also been listed.

## Maps

Grid references can all be found in the Ordnance Survey, Landranger and Pathfinder series. Landranger sheets 144, 154, 155, 156 and 169 cover all the walks in this volume.

## Security

Suffolk Police continually warn the public to be aware of thieves breaking into cars, especially at isolated car-parks. Motorists are strongly advised to leave all valuables locked in the boot.

Lavenham (route 12)

# Map symbols

|  |  |  |  |
|--------|-------------|--------|-------------|
| →—→ | Route | ═══ | Road |
| ⟳⟳⟳⟳⟳ | Shortened route | --------- | Track or bridleway |
| ∼∼∼ | River or stream | 🌊 | Pond or lake |
| ▪▪ | Settlement | ⟍⟍ | Bridge |
| ✝ | Church | ■ | Building |
| ❀❀❀❀ | Deciduous woodland | ♠♠♠♠ | Coniferous woodland |
| ⟍⟍⟍⟍ | Steep bank | START | Start of walk |
| P H | Public House | C P | Car Park |
| ② | Number corresponding with directions | ⚐ | Golf course |
| | | ✗ | Windmill |

# Dunwich

## Outline
St James Street – Sandy Lane – Mount Pleasant Farm – Greyfriars Wood – Cliff Path – Greyfriars Friary – Car-park

## Summary
This walk explores the area around the small village of Dunwich, or rather what's left of it. For centuries erosion has claimed a metre of land every year. The coastal path has to be frequently diverted away from the crumbling cliffs. Other parts of the route include heathland, ancient trackways, woodland and monastic remains. The cliff path gives excellent views of landmarks in Walberswick and Southwold further along the coast.

## Attractions
Dunwich, the ancient capital of East Anglia, was once the seat of a bishopric. Economic decline started in 1328 when raging storms threw shingle into large heaps and blocked the harbour. As a result Dunwich lost its sea trade to nearby ports of Walberswick and Southwold and never recovered. Over the centuries coastal erosion has accounted for the disappearance of numerous buildings and churches beneath the waves. All Saints, the last of the old Dunwich churches, finally toppled over the cliffs as recently as 1920. In 1992 pounding north-easterly storms took away 5 metres of cliff near the wall of 13th century Greyfriars Monastery which marked the boundary of this once great town.

Much of the history of Dunwich, including the Roman and Saxon periods, is documented in the museum which is housed in a row of cottages in St James Street. The main gallery upstairs is devoted to local wildlife and social history. Youngsters no doubt will be fascinated by a display of stuffed birds and mammals.

Sandy Lane is thought to be a pre-Roman track connecting the town to the interior of the county. Likewise the track leading to the cliff top known as Middle-Ditch, may have been an old road which led into ancient Dunwich.

In springtime the water meadows are ablaze with colourful buttercups and campion, and in autumn the tall hedgerows and brambles produce a natural store of fruit such as blackberries, bullaces and sloes. The light sandy soil covered mainly by bracken, heather and gorse provides a natural habitat for birds and other forms of wildlife.

The Franciscan Friary was in use from the late 13th century until the dissolution of the monasteries in the 1530s when it passed into secular ownership. Nowadays the remains include a gateway and the surviving wall of what was once the refectory. You can look inside the compound which often includes a selection of livestock and ponies.

*continued on page 14*

11

# Route 1

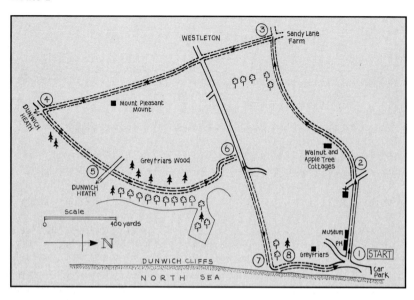

Monastic remains, Dunwich

12

# Route 1

## Dunwich $3\frac{1}{2}$ miles

### Start

*The village of Dunwich lies just off the B1125 and is signposted from the A12 north of Yoxford. Follow the signs to the beach car-park (GR 480707).*

### Route

1. From the car-park turn right onto the road into St James Street and walk down towards the church.

2. At the road junction beside the church, go straight across to join a gravel track between two tall hedgerows. Past Walnut and Apple Tree cottages the path becomes grassy and leads through a small wood before reaching Sandy Lane farm.

3. Turn left at the farm and walk up the track until you reach the Dunwich to Westleton road. Cross the road and follow the wide track to Mount Pleasant farm.

4. A quarter mile past the farm buildings the track reaches a junction. (If you wish to make a detour to Dunwich Heath follow the path to the right.) Otherwise turn left here and follow this path with bracken on either side until you reach a road.

5. At the junction with the road turn right and walk a few yards before turning left onto a footpath. Keep on the path which takes you into Greyfriars Wood.

6. When you exit from the wood you will find the Dunwich to Westleton road again. Turn right and continue down the road. Where the road bends left go straight ahead onto a track and pass under a small bridge before arriving at the cliff edge.

7. Turn left along the cliff path. There are several short diversions along this section as a result of erosion of the sea cliffs.

8. Follow any diversion signs which will eventually lead to some monastic remains. Once at the road turn right, walk down the hill and rediscover the car-park.

Amongst the thorn bushes near the cliff top is at least one remaining gravestone, it stands in memory of Jacob Forster who died in 1796 aged 58. The gravestone is getting perilously near the cliff edge. How long before it too disappears?

A short detour from the route near Mount Pleasant Farm will take you to Dunwich Heath. This is a spot owned by the National Trust and well known for its scenic beauty. From here a path leads to the RSPB's famous bird sanctuary at Minsmere.

**Public Transport**
Dunwich is not served by public transport. Nearest BR station is Darsham 5 miles away.

**Refreshments**
Flora Tea Rooms is beside the beach car-park. It gets quite crowded in the summer time, especially at weekends when visitors flock from miles around to savour its locally famous fish and chips. Pub meals and picnic tables are available at the Ship Inn in St James Street.

# Framlingham

## Outline
Framlingham Castle – Castle Meadow – Badingham Road – Great Lodge Farms – Playing Fields – Mere – Castle.

## Summary
This walk starts and finishes beside the superb 12th century Framlingham castle which is in the care of English Heritage. Entry to the castle itself is well worth the entrance fee.

The remainder of the walk takes in a mere and nature reserve. For those who wish to walk a little further, arable farmland, a stretch of metalled road and playing fields are added to the route. The grey walls of the castle and its massive earthworks dominate the landscape and can be seen to good effect more or less throughout the walk. However, probably the best scenic view is from across the reed-fringed mere.

## Attractions
Framlingham has one of the best-preserved and most-visited castles in England. For centuries it belonged to the notorious and quarrelsome Bigod family. The castle was built in the 12th century by Roger Bigod, Earl of Norfolk, on the site of a motte and bailey castle destroyed by Henry II. Instead of using the traditional Norman keep and bailey design, Bigod introduced a new style of castle featuring a continuous curtain wall linking 13 towers. Today the structure from the castle outside looks almost the same as when it was built. Children, if accompanied by an adult, can climb the spiral staircase and walk around the battlements. The summit gives a bird's eye view of the castle interior which includes a museum and a bookshop.

The small nature reserve beside the mere is administered by the Suffolk Wildlife Trust. Depending on the time of year, cattle graze on the reserve in order to keep vegetation short and thereby create a herb-rich meadowland which in turn will hopefully encourage insects and small mammals along with birds such as snipe and barn owl.

The castle mere was dug out in about 1190 and its water regularly attracts a wide variety of wildfowl which dart amongst the reeds and marsh marigolds. Almost opposite the car-park entrance is a small pond which is a great favourite with youngsters who wish to feed the mallard ducks.

**Route 2**

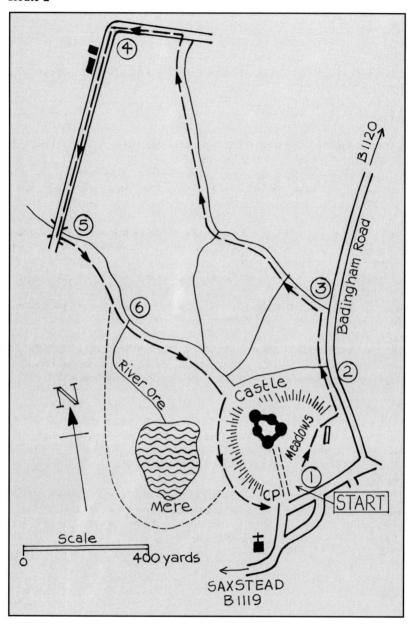

# Route 2

## Framlingham                                                    2 miles

### Start
At Framlingham, which lies south of the A1120 about 15 miles east of Stowmarket. Drive past Market Hill to the Castle car-park (GR 285636).

### Route
1. From the car-park look for the white gate and enter Castle Meadows with the castle on your left. Bear right through the gap in the hedgerow into Town Meadows. Pass through the metal gate into Badingham Road.

2. Turn left along the road for 75 yards, then turn left down small steps into an arable field.

3. Follow the hedge and cross over a ditch and continue along the field edge, gradually bearing right. After $\frac{3}{4}$ mile, turn left at the road and walk down the hill for 150 yards.

4. At the bottom of the hill, turn left with farm buildings on your right.

5. After walking half a mile, turn left at a bridge and cross over a stream. Soon after cross over a footbridge and enter a playing field.

6. Walk beside the field edge and eventually cross over a bridge and stile. You have the choice of turning right or left. Either turning will take you round past the mere and nature reserve and finally back to the car-park via Castle Meadows.


### Public Transport
Eastern Counties operates a service from Woodbridge and Ipswich. Nearest BR station is Wickham Market 9 miles away.

### Refreshments
Castle Inn next to the car-park offers teas and coffee. Otherwise refreshments can be obtained from public houses and cafes in the town. Framlingham Castle is open Good Friday or 1 April (whichever is earlier) to 30 September: Open Daily 10 am–6 pm. 1 October to Maundy Thursday or 31 March (whichever is earlier): Open Tuesday to Sunday 10 am–4 pm.

Sculptures by Barbara Hepworth, the River Alde in the background

# Iken and the River Alde

**Outline**
Iken – River Alde – Estuary – Snape Maltings – Iken.

**Summary**
Anyone who wants to walk in picturesque surroundings unspoilt by random development will enjoy this undemanding walk. The route above all is noted for magnificent views of the River Alde and its estuary. If the river wall has been breached by high tides, you may find the path nearest the river impassable. However, it's worth re-tracing your footsteps for part of the return journey if only for the distant views of Iken church isolated on a cliff high above the water's edge. The sloping car-park also gives superb views of the river and estuary. The local beauty spot of Iken Cliff is nearby and worth a visit.

**Attractions**
Although the estuary at Snape Bridge is only 5 miles from the sea, the Alde meanders around several Suffolk villages, taking some 20 miles to reach the coast. At Orfordness the Alde becomes the Ore as it flows alongside an 11 mile shingle spit before entering the North Sea at Shingle Street. In former times sailing barges used the river to ply their cargoes of malt and coal to and from the inland port of Snape, the highest point a vessel of any size can navigate up the estuary. Nowadays the barges are not so numerous and apart from the odd pleasure craft there is little to disturb the estuary and its birdlife.

Soon after commencing the walk you become aware of relative peace and stillness save for the movement and call of wading birds and the breeze rustling through the tall reedbeds. At low tide the river is a mere trickle of freshwater, revealing creeks and saltmarshes. The brackish combination of fresh and salt water attracts sheluck, redshank and the occasional avocet in their search for food. Parties of dunlin wheeling left and right against the changing light make an impressive sight. Parts of the walk pass through reedbeds and where necessary old railway sleepers have been laid to carry walkers over squelching mud.

The outline of Snape maltings looms closer as the walk progresses. In 1854 a local Victorian businessman named Newson Garrett began his malting industry here. In their heyday the maltings were one of the largest in East Anglia. Malt, made from Suffolk barley, was shipped down the Alde to breweries as far away as Norwich and London. Incidentally, Newson Garrett's daughter, Elizabeth Garrett Anderson, became the first woman to qualify as a doctor in Britain.

Nowadays the Maltings have been converted to a far different use. Pride of place must go to the world-famous Snape Concert Hall, a former malt house. The unique acoustics of this building attract international artists and the nearby Britten–Pears music school provides tuition for up and coming young musicians.

*continued on page 22*

19

# Route 3

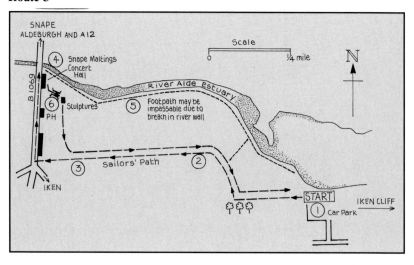

Dunlin in summer plumage

# Route 3

## Iken and the River Alde                                      3 miles

### Start
*At Iken, about 4 miles due east of Aldeburgh and on the south side of the River Alde estuary. From the A12 Ipswich to Lowestoft road turn off onto the A1094 (GR 398564).*

### Route
1. *Proceed to bottom left-hand corner of car-park and follow the waymarked path, with farmland on the left and the river on the right.*

2. *The path passes through reedbeds. In parts, walking is over railway sleepers to avoid mud underneath.*

3. *When you come to a fork in the path bear left and head for the B1069 road. Turn right and follow the pavement to Snape Maltings. Locals say the road bridge over the river is actually in Tunstall.*

4. *After exploring the Maltings proceed through the car-park, and find a path beside the riverwall. You may find this path is impassable due to the riverwall being breached further ahead.*

5. *If the path is passable continue on the path beside the river and after about ¾ mile bear right through reedbeds to rejoin the path back to the car-park.*

6. *If the path is impassable come out of the Maltings car-park, cross over a wooden footbridge and walk past sculptures. Bear right and follow the path till you rejoin the original path. Turn left and re-trace your steps back to the car-park.*

### Public Transport
Transport none.

### Refreshments
The Plough and Sail in Snape does bar meals and a Sunday carvery. Snacks and cups of tea can be obtained in the Maltings complex.

Elsewhere you can browse amongst renovated buildings which house craft shops and art galleries. Near the Concert Hall you may be surprised to see an arrangement of sculptures by Barbara Hepworth. From an adjacent quay it's possible to take a pleasure trip on the Alde. Departures between April and October are dependent on tidal times.

Snape Maltings and sculptures

# Waldringfield

## Outline
Maybush Inn – River foreshore – Sailing Clubhouse – White Hall – Mill Road – Maybush Inn.

## Summary
The small village of Waldringfield is uncommercialised and retains the atmosphere of a bygone age; yet it's only a few miles away from the international container port of Felixstowe. Its close proximity to the River Deben ensures its popularity with members of the sailing fraternity.

The circuit, which includes some gentle uphill walking, begins on the sandy foreshore and heads inland before returning to the village. From vantage points in the car-park and from higher ground in the fields, grand views of the river and the immediate landscape can be obtained.

## Attractions
The River Deben runs through about 10 miles of picturesque countryside from its estuary at Felixstowe Ferry up to the town of Woodbridge. In former times the Deben was something of a mini industrial waterway, carrying cargoes of farm produce to towns and cities and returning with coal and bricks. Nowadays the river is used mainly for leisure purposes. A thriving sailing club organises a series of local racing regattas.

The area gets quite crowded, especially in the summer, with locals mixing with holiday sailors. Boats of all shapes and sizes appear to be everywhere. Indeed, driving down the hill towards the river you almost run straight into a boat repair yard before turning sharp into the car-park entrance. Not surprisingly perhaps, this walk takes on a nautical flavour.

Notices on the foreshore caution boat owners to be aware of bathers and children. Should children wish to venture to the water's edge, anxious parents can keep watch from seats positioned on the shore.

Paths crossing fields which contain crops such as corn and sugar beet, are well-worn and can easily be followed. Although the light soil can be tacky on occasions, it is not as bad as clay soil which seems to cling permanently to footwear. After periods of heavy rainfall water is often slow to drain away, leaving large puddles and intricate patterns on the surface. By contrast during periods of severe drought, you may come across irrigation machinery dispersing bursts of water onto thirsty soil.

The walk can be slightly extended to allow children to visit a play area or kick a ball around a playing field. A small amusement area can also be found in a corner of the car-park. For those who wish to conclude their visit with a pleasure trip on the Deben, the *M.V. Jahan* departs from Waldringfield during May to October.

23

# Route 4

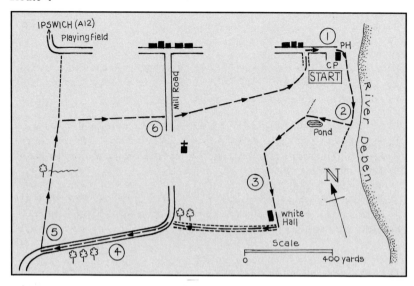

Boats at anchor on the River Deben

# Route 4

## Waldringfield $2\frac{1}{2}$ miles

### Start

At Waldringfield on the River Deben 8 miles east of Ipswich and 6 miles south of Woodbridge. From the A12 take an unclassified road to the village. Car-park is to the rear of the Maybush Inn (GR 287447).

### Route

1. Pass the Maybush Inn and turn right onto the sandy foreshore. Walk past the Sailing Clubhouse. Pass a few beach huts, then quickly swing right and left past a boat compound.

2. Ignore a path going straight ahead and bear right. The narrow path passes between hedges for 150 yards. Soon a small reservoir comes into view. Bear left where the track meets the pond on the right. Head straight for a path which leads to a field entrance.

3. Proceed across the field. Rising ground gives superb views of the river to your left. Keep in the middle of the field and eventually meet a grassy path beside White Hall. Turn right at the end of the path and proceed along a bridleway. Walk along the bridleway to a junction with a metalled road.

4. Turn left at the road and follow it for $\frac{3}{4}$ mile. Where the road bears left follow a footpath sign into a field just past an electricity pole.

5. Head straight across the field on a well-worn path. Tall buildings in the distance on the left belong to British Telecom. After 400 yards the path enters an enclosure of bracken and brambles. Walk ahead for 100 yards and turn right through a gap and continue on a path beside the hedge.

6. Cross Mill Road and follow a path across another field. Look for an exit in the lower left-hand corner. Bear left and follow a track to the road. Walk downhill and rediscover the car-park entrance on the right.

### Public Transport

Eastern Counties buses run from Woodbridge and Ipswich.

### Refreshments

The Maybush public house has tables in a riverside garden. A village shop sells ice cream and soft drinks.

Monastic remains, Dunwich (route 1)

# Trimley St Mary

**Outline**

Searsons Farm – River Orwell – Nature Reserve – Sleighton Hill – Loompit Lake – Grimston Hall – Searsons Farm.

**Summary**

The first part of the walk explores the approach to the River Orwell. The huge lifting cranes which dominate the landscape bear witness to the port of Felixstowe's rapid expansion programme. From the riverbank extensive views of the Shotley Peninsula, Harwich and the Essex border can be obtained. Apart from two short inclines at Sleighton Hill and above Loompit Lake, walking is easy and straightforward. A short detour enables visitors to obtain a panoramic view of port operations at Felixstowe. Pushchairs are not recommended for all of the walk although it is possible to take them as far as the dock viewing area at Fagbury Cliff. After the walk you may care to visit the beach at Felixstowe which is only 15 minutes away by car or public transport.

**Attractions**

The River Orwell is nowadays a maritime highway for ships sailing mainly between the Continent and to the inland port of Ipswich. The walk follows the riverbank for some two miles. On the way you may spot the odd Thames sailing barge making its leisurely way on the ebb tide. At Levington there is a yachting marina and in the distance lies the local beauty spot of Pin Mill.

The nature reserve at Trimley St. Mary was paid for by Felixstowe Port as part of its Parliamentary permission, to help compensate for the loss of feeding and breeding grounds for rare birds destroyed in the port expansion. The site, managed by Suffolk Wildlife Trust, was previously arable land but has been transformed into a network of dykes and lagoons for all types of wildlife. The reserve has a visitor centre and five bird hides which are open to the public.

The growth of Felixstowe Port has been nothing short of phenomenal. From being a small dock basin in the 1950s it has grown to become the biggest handler of container traffic in the UK. Adults as well as youngsters will find it worthwhile to make a detour to the dock viewing area at Fagbury Cliff. From a position high up on the cliff, giant gantry cranes can be seen unloading container boxes with forklift trucks and juggernaut lorries busy distributing their loads around the quayside.

Just above Sleighton Hill at Levington, boats can be seen tied up at a large marina. Past Loompit Lake, which caters for private fishing, there are some of the best views of the river looking towards Pin Mill. The walk passes Grimston Hall, birthplace of Thomas Cavendish, the second Englishman to circumnavigate the world. Legend has it that as a boy Cavendish played by the Orwell watching the ships. He set out on his voyage round the world from Harwich, just across the water, in 1586.

# Route 5

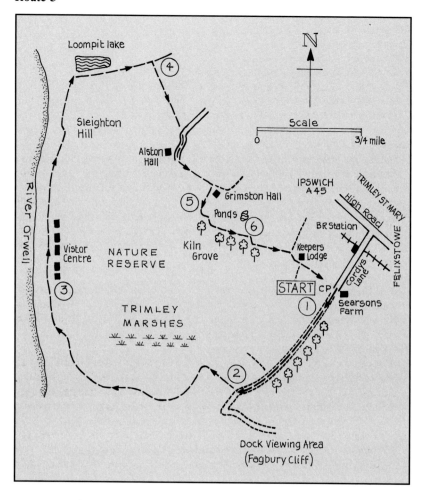

# Route 5

## Trimley St Mary **5 miles**

### Start

*Trimley St. Mary lies just off the A45 west of Felixstowe. Take signposted slip road and head for the village High Road. From High Road turn into Station Road and cross over a level crossing. Go down Cordys Lane and park adjacent to Searsons Farm where there is an official car-park area (GR 278358).*

### Route

1. *Go straight down a bridleway towards the river for $\frac{3}{4}$mile. Ignore the first right turn. Proceed to the next right turn signposted to the nature reserve. (A short detour straight ahead and up the hill will bring you to Fagbury Cliff viewing area.)*

2. *Turn right here. With a steep mound of earth on your left follow a track until you reach the river wall. You have the choice of walking on the wall itself or on the bridleway. Look behind you at this stage and see the huge quayside cranes and the port.*

3. *Bird hides and the reserve visitor centre will soon appear on the right. Continue ahead and a boat marina will come into view. The track bears left and then right to rise above sandy cliffs at Sleighton Hill. At Loompit Lake, turn right up a sandy track. Superb views of the river can be had here.*

4. *At the top of the track turn right after passing through a gate. Continue on the track and eventually turn right onto a tarmac road towards Alston Hall. Once level with the Hall, turn left and head for Grimston Hall. When you reach the latter do not go through the farmyard but follow the path and bear to the right.*

5. *After walking 400 yards along a field edge, bear left into Kiln Grove. The path goes downhill through a spinney and then swings left and right by a pond. After 20 yards the path turns left and proceeds uphill. A wooden seat is conveniently placed at the top for a rest and views of the marshes.*

6. *The path continues through a plantation of young trees. When you meet a crossroads in the path, ignore it and carry on straight ahead, passing Keepers Cottage on your left. Soon a gap will appear in the hedge. Go through the gap and continue on a gravel path, which will bring you to Searsons Farm.*

**Public Transport**
There is a BR station at Trimley St. Mary, five minutes' walk from Searsons Farm. Eastern Counties buses from Ipswich stop nearby in the High Road.


**Refreshments**
Meals and bar snacks are available at the Three Mariners public house near the churches in the High Road.

Orwell Bridge (Suffolk County Council)

# Pipers Vale

### Outline
Pipers Vale – Orwell Bridge – River Estuary – Pond Hall Farm – Pipers Vale.

### Summary
Situated on the eastern bank of the River Orwell, Pipers Vale is one of the last areas of natural countryside left in the town of Ipswich. This amenity, besides being special to local people, provides the visitor with a short walk through a vale which gives attractive views of a river estuary, wading birds, cliffs, shore and farmland. Dominating the route is the massive structure of the Orwell road bridge. Thomas Gainsborough, the famous landscape artist, used the area around the Vale as a backdrop for some of his paintings and nowadays his name is perpetuated by a nearby housing estate.

### Attractions
As you proceed down the Vale amongst the gorse bushes, you follow a track which was used as an access road when the Orwell Bridge was built. Opened in 1982 the bridge is 4218 feet long and the longest pre-stressed concrete centre span stands 623 feet high. Youngsters can race ahead and stand under the bridge as the road traffic roars overhead. Sad to say some of the columns are daubed with ugly graffiti. The building to the right with its three tall chimneys is the former coal-fired Cliff Quay power station.

Past the bridge the path runs gently down to the estuary shore. As the tide recedes hundreds of wildfowl flock to the food-rich mudflats. You can get within easy focusing distance of wading birds running to and fro and probing the grey ooze with their curved bills. A telescope would be useful to help differentiate between the various species and seasonal plumage.

Visible on the opposite bank is Freston Tower. The real reason for which the tower was built remains unclear. Popular opinion suggests that it was originally an early Elizabethan folly or used perhaps as a look-out by smugglers. Another version is that it was built so the owner's daughter, Ellen De Freston, could study a different subject each day in the six tower rooms.

The walk also provides views of ships entering and departing from the port of Ipswich. Look up and you may see parachutists falling towards their dropping zone at the nearby airport. An added bonus for youngsters is the possible sighting of animals during the walk through Pond Hall Farm farmyard.

**Route 6**

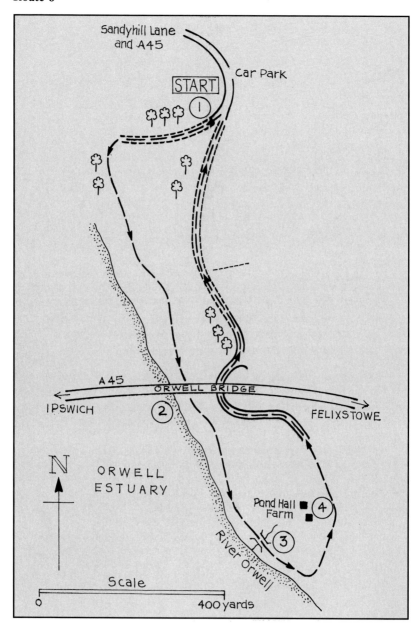

# Route 6

## Pipers Vale

**2 miles**

### Start

*Come off the A45 at Ipswich and follow signposted route to airport. Pass the small airport perimeter and after ½ mile turn left into Maryon Road. Continue past the sports centre and Gainsborough housing estate before entering Landseer Road. Go down this road and turn left at bottom of the hill into Sandyhill Lane. Continue along road to car-park (GR 177416).*

### Route

1. *From the car-park walk a short distance and enter Pipers Vale. Continue walking down a track past gorse bushes. The path heads for and eventually passes under Orwell bridge.*

2. *Continue on a well-worn path along the top of a sandy cliff. Soon the path gently descends towards the estuary.*

3. *Cross a stream via a concrete pipe bridge and walk alongside the river. After a short distance, turn left on a path facing away from the estuary. Climb a stile and follow a track through Pond Hall Farm.*

4. *Continue ahead, join a section of road and pass beneath the bridge. Proceed up the hill and bear left beside an old oak tree. The path returns through the Vale and back to the car-park.*

### Public Transport

A number 21 bus from Ipswich town centre takes you closest to Pipers Vale. Alight in Romney Road on the Gainsborough Estate.

### Refreshments

Pipers Vale public house in Sandyhill Road.

Male blackcap

# Christchurch Park

**Outline**
Christchurch Mansion – Round Pond – Wilderness Pond – Water Meadow –
Mayors' Avenue – Park Avenue – Christchurch Mansion.

**Summary**
Municipal parks are sometimes overlooked as a source of circular walks. Ipswich is
particularly fortunate in having a superb park only a few minutes walk from the
town centre. Christchurch Park, which was first opened to the public in 1895,
nowadays satisfies the needs of recreation and conservation. This walk amongst
undulating parkland encounters interesting features such as a mansion cum
museum, centuries-old trees, a water-meadow, bird reserve, duck ponds, arboretum
and a whole lot more. For youngsters there is a large slide, a play area with a Wild
West theme and an opportunity to watch and feed the ducks.

**Attractions**
As you enter the park entrance in Soane Street the first thing you notice is the
imposing Christchurch Mansion. The children may want to make a quick dash to
the duck pond, but a delay is worthwhile in order to take a rewarding look inside
this building which is full of historic interest. Although nowadays the mansion
functions as a museum with collections of early oak furniture, portraits of royalty
and local gentry and household effects of bygone years, its origin was quite
different. As Lord of the Manor of Christchurch, Edmund Withypool in 1548
began building a handsome house on the site of a former priory and named it
Christchurch Mansion. Two centuries later in 1735 the estate was taken over by
Claude Fonnereau, a wealthy London merchant of Huguenot descent. Members of
the Fonnereau family lived in the house until 1892 when the estate was put up for
sale. The park and the mansion were saved from dispersal by a wealthy banker and
local brewer, Felix Thornley Cobbold, who generously presented it to the borough
of Ipswich in 1895.

Standing either side of the park's central avenue are pollarded oaks and sweet
chestnuts which are reckoned to be at least 300–400 years old. They managed to
survive the '87 hurricane but 235 other trees were lost. Since that fateful day a
careful replanting programme has taken place. Evidence of the latter can be seen in
the Mayors' Avenue where each year the town's mayor plants a young sapling
during his or her term of office. Elsewhere a bird reserve attracts such species as
nuthatch, blackcap, woodpecker and tawny owl. Bird watchers will find this area
particularly rewarding, especially during the early springtime.

The round and wilderness ponds contain a mixture of wild and captive
waterfowl. Mallard ducks are in abundance and are always on the lookout for

*continued on page 38*

**Route 7**

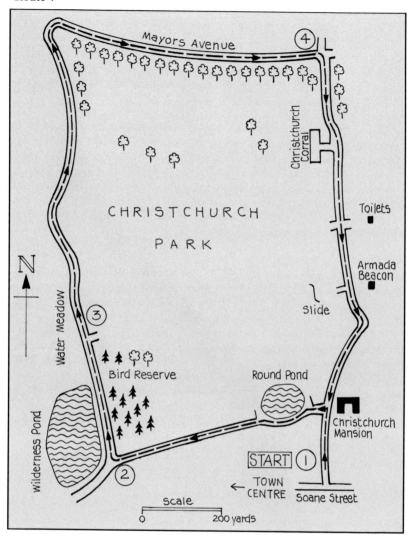

# Route 7

## Christchurch Park $1\frac{1}{2}$ miles

### Start

At Christchurch Park, in Ipswich on the south side of the town. The main entrance to the park is in Soane Street. Restricted and unrestricted car parking is permitted in areas around the exterior of the park (GR 165448).

### Route

1. From Soane Street entrance follow the path towards the mansion. Bear left to visit the Round and Wilderness ponds.

2. Turn right at Wilderness Pond. Keep straight ahead with pond railings on your left and trees on the right. The water-meadow will shortly appear on the left.

3. Carry on for 500 yards and turn right into Mayors' Avenue.

4. At the end of the avenue turn right into Park Avenue. The children's 'Wild West' play area will shortly appear on the right. Carry on downhill past the mansion and head for the main gate.

### Public Transport

Christchurch Park is within easy walking distance from the town centre. The main entrance is in Soane Street.

### Refreshments

Kiosks in the park serve light refreshments such as teas, soft drinks and ice cream. There are lots of food and drink establishments in the town.

youngsters with titbits to feed them. Other occasional visitors, depending on the time of year, include black headed gulls, tufted and pochard duck, kingfishers and herons.

Situated in other odd corners of the park is a Boer War statue, memorials to Protestant Martyrs and to the fallen of both World Wars. Near the putting green is an Armada Beacon erected and lit in 1988 to celebrate 400 years since the defeat of the Spanish fleet. Besides feeding and watching the ducks youngsters will want to visit the Christchurch Corral – a Wild West theme play area. With acres of grassland present there is plenty of room to kick a ball or fly a kite.

Christchurch Mansion

# Flatford and Constable Country

## Outline
Flatford – River Stour – Dedham Vale – Fen Bridge – Rare Breeds Centre – Dedham Mill – Gosnalds Farm – Flatford.

## Summary
Much of this walk takes place in 'Constable Country', so named after one of England's greatest landscape painters, John Constable. Although much of the landscape familiar to Constable has long since disappeared, it's still possible to identify the sites where he painted such pictures as *The Haywain*, *The Leaping Horse* and *Dedham Mill*. The walk passes through lush water-meadows beside the quiet waters of the River Stour before leading to a sneak preview of Dedham just across the Essex border. For children there is an opportunity to visit a rare breeds animal park and play a game of pooh sticks on Flatford Bridge.

## Attractions
With Flatford's increasing popularity a one-way traffic system is in operation to cope with traffic congestion on narrow roads leading to the car-park. The latter is pleasantly landscaped with conveniently placed picnic tables.

As you walk away from the car-park towards Flatford Bridge, a short detour will take you to Flatford Mill and Willy Lott's Cottage. The mill was built in about 1733 to grind wheat into flour using water power. A substantial Suffolk farmhouse built around 1600 was subsequently lived in by a yeoman farmer named Willy Lott, and later became known as Willy Lott's cottage. The viewpoint from which Constable painted *The Hay Wain* is by the left-hand gatepost, looking across the pool. On the bridge over the River Stour children can indulge in a game of pooh sticks. There are usually a number of mallard ducks in the vicinity looking for scraps of food. Call in at nearby thatched Bridge Cottage and you can order teas and obtain details of boat hire.

The walk continues beside the Stour as it meanders its way through lush water-meadows in Dedham Vale. The presence of cattle is a reminder that farmers still retain traditional grazing methods in the Vale. Willow trees overlook the grassy riverbanks giving a scene of peace and tranquillity. Anyone with a penchant for sketching and painting will find the area very rewarding.

Younger children especially will enjoy the visit to Dedham Rare Breeds Park. The farm is home to a comprehensive collection of rare farm animals which were once common on farms throughout the country. Between wide grass walkways the animals can be watched in natural surroundings. Children can stroke the bristly backs of pigs and cuddle baby rabbits. Those with tired toddlers may wish to fetch their cars and park in the free car-park to collect their children.

*continued on page 42*

# Route 8

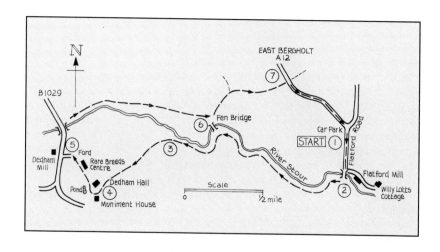

Feeding time, Rare Breeds Park, Dedham

# Route 8

## Flatford and Constable Country                                    4 miles

### Start

*At Flatford, just south of East Bergholt, which is just east of the A12 midway between Colchester and Ipswich. From East Bergholt take the narrow road to Flatford (GR 077335).*

### Route

1. *From the car-park proceed downhill to Flatford Bridge. A detour can be made to the Mill and Willy Lott's cottage.*

2. *Cross the bridge and a stile and turn right onto the path beside the river. After ¾ mile pass Fen Bridge and continue on the well-worn path. Cross over a stile which takes you over a water channel.*

3. *The path to Dedham shortly crosses a field. The route is marked by white-painted bands on posts. Cross over a stile and continue with the animal park on your right. Near Dedham Hall the path becomes a wide track and continues past farm buildings before finishing at Muniment House.*

4. *At a junction with an unmarked road turn sharp right into the lane. Keep straight ahead and gradually bear left onto a path. Cross over a stile with a large pond on the left. Carry on, cross over a stile and pass the entrance to Dedham Rare Breeds Park. Just after crossing another stile cross a footbridge over the ford and walk to the top of the lane.*

5. *At the junction with the B1029 turn right and continue walking towards and eventually pass over the river bridge. Turn right, go down steps and find a path beside the river. Keep on the path and eventually climb over 3 stiles in fairly quick succession.*

6. *At Fen Bridge the path bears left and then joins a track which passes over a water course. Ignore the left fork, keep on the track, which bends to the right, and cross over a metal stile. Carry on up the path through a meadow.*

7. *At the top of the meadow cross the East Bergholt to Flatford road and find a path on the other side of the hedge. Continue downhill, passing the entrance to a sewage works. When the path finishes at the bottom of the hill, join a metalled road and continue for another 250 yards. The car-park will appear on the right-hand side.*

Dedham is a small town which derived considerable prosperity from the medieval cloth industry. Constable attended the former grammar school in the High Street. Mill House, facing the Mill, was once the home of his sister, Mary Whalley.

Towards the end of the walk as you reach the top of a hill, look back over your shoulder. Beneath you is a panoramic view of Dedham Vale, justifiably designated as an 'Area of Outstanding Natural Beauty'.

**Public Transport**
Eastern Counties run to East Bergholt and there is then an approximately 1 mile walk to Flatford. Nearest BR station Manningtree. (Footpath adjacent to station will take you to Flatford.)

**Refreshments**
Teas available at Bridge Cottage. Sweets, ice creams and soft drinks available at kiosk situated before bridge. Selection of tea shops and public houses in Dedham.

Willy Lott's cottage, Flatford

42

# Hadleigh

## Outline
Toppersfield Bridge – Broom Hill Nature Reserve – Friars Hill – Coram Street – Corks Lane – Riverside – Toppersfield Bridge.

## Summary
An interesting and compact walk centred in and around the historic market town of Hadleigh. Starting and finishing at the small car-park adjacent to medieval Toppersfield Bridge, the route features a delightful riverside walk. Other attractions include a ramble through open countryside and a visit to a nature reserve. The walk also skirts the top of a cricket field and passes a children's play area. The going is quite easy especially where the path is made up beside the river. Elsewhere paths can get rather muddy, particularly after periods of heavy rain.

## Attractions
The centre-piece of the walk is a half mile stretch of path which runs alongside the River Brett. Besides linking picturesque villages such as Chelsworth and Monks Eleigh, the Brett was once an important water source for the medieval woollen cloth industry which played such a decisive role in Hadleigh's early prosperity. The route passes through an avenue of trees which provide shade during sunny weather and a colourful display of falling leaves in autumn time. Between the trees there is an occasional glimpse of the lead spire on St Mary's church. The timber-framed Guildhall along with the Deanery Tower, which at one time was meant to be a gateway to a larger residence near the river, are only a short distance and are well worth visiting.

Walking beside the headland of an arable field brings you to Broom Hill Nature Reserve. Hadleigh is fortunate in having such a quiet place so close to the town centre. The reserve, comprising almost 10 acres, is managed by Babergh District Council. Rabbits help keep the grass short and a large area of dense blackthorn provides nesting cover for woodland and garden birds. Also part of the reserve is a disused quarry which formerly supplied bricks to local industry. A climb up a steep path is rewarded at the top by a panoramic view of the town and the surrounding Brett valley.

The path passes between the town's cemetery and cricket ground. On certain days in summer you can hear the crack of leather on willow. You may care to linger awhile and let energetic children amuse themselves at a nearby play area which includes swings, slide, see-saw and climbing frame.

Back near the car-park tables sited on a raised bank provide the opportunity to finish the walk off with a picnic.

**Route 9**

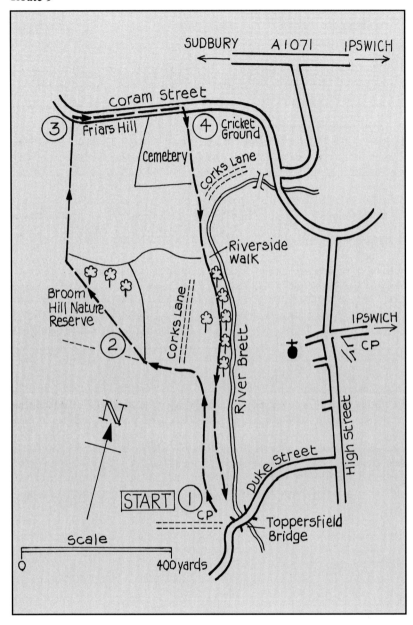

## Route 9

### Hadleigh

**2 miles**

#### Start

*Hadleigh is 9 miles west of Ipswich and can be approached by the A1071 and A134/
A1071 from Sudbury. From High Street turn into Duke Street and drive over
Toppersfield Bridge into the adjacent car-park (GR 021425).*

#### Route

1. *From the car-park follow a sign marked Constitution Hill and Bridge Street and
   proceed alongside field edge. Ignore the path leading to Corks Lane unless you wish
   to go direct to the riverside.*

2. *Keep on the original path and enter Broom Hill Nature Reserve. Carry on through
   the reserve and find a path which leads to the top. Find the exit in a corner and turn
   right into the field headland. Continue on the path before swinging right and left
   through an entrance to an adjoining field.*

3. *Walk 20 yards and descend steps with caution onto a metalled road. Turn right and
   walk down Friars Hill for 120 yards to Coram Street.*

4. *Turn right onto a path running between the cricket ground and the cemetery. Look
   for the children's play area in the corner. Proceed up Corks Lane for the start of the
   entrance to riverside walk. Walk beside the river and back to the car-park.*

#### Public Transport

Eastern Counties, C. J. Partridge & Sons, and Rules Coaches operate transport to
Hadleigh.

#### Refreshments

There are plenty of refreshment outlets in and around the town. A pleasant
alternative would be to use the picnic table site near the river.

Needham Lake

Ringed plover

46

# Needham Market and the Gipping Valley

**Outline**

Station yard – Lakeside – Mill Lane – Darmsden – Pipps Ford – Gipping Valley Footpath – Station Yard.

**Summary**

The Gipping Valley runs between Ipswich and Stowmarket and follows the course of the River Gipping. Although it's possible to walk the full 17 miles of towpath, this walk concentrates on a small section in the Needham Market area. The route also visits the lake, Mill Lane and the tiny hamlet of Darmsden.

Older children will find the walk easy going and interesting but for youngsters a circular walk around the lake might prove sufficient.

**Attractions**

In former times the station yard, from where the walk starts, was a place where corn was milled and coal bagged up from trucks held in railway sidings. The BR station still remains but nowadays the yard is a mixture of small businesses and shops. Adults will have to bend their backs as they enter the narrow tunnel which runs under the railway line. Children will have no such problem although they may be wary of the noise as an occasional train thunders overhead.

The 11-acre lake at Needham Market is popular with locals and tourists alike. There is a free car-park and tables available for picnicking. Youngsters can feed the ducks or sail a model boat. On certain days instruction is available for water-based activities such as angling and canoeing. At the top end of the lake an area consisting of grassland and muddy lagoons has been set aside as a haven for wildlife. Halfway up Mill Lane there is a deep pit where chalk is extracted and processed as lime for agricultural purposes. The mill from which the lane takes its name has long since gone with no visible signs remaining.

A mile or so from the old A45 lies the small hamlet of Darmsden. A no-through road leads to Tarston Hall and a few isolated cottages. Iron Age pottery dating from 600–400 BC has been found here. Standing alone on a hill is the little church of St. Andrew. This former medieval church was totally rebuilt in 1880 and finally declared redundant in 1979.

The ridge above the valley gives a panoramic view of the whole area. There are superb views of local villages such as Creeting, Coddenham and Barham. Bosmere Hall, associated with the great botanist Sir Samuel Uvedale, stands out as does the Italianate appearance of Shrubland Hall, former home of the De Saumarez family and nowadays an up-market health clinic.

Near Pipps Ford the walk joins up with the Gipping Valley Footpath. With low rainfall and increasing commercial abstraction, nowadays the Gipping often takes on a slow and shallow appearance. However, the river supports a diverse habitat.

*continued on page 50*

47

## Route 10

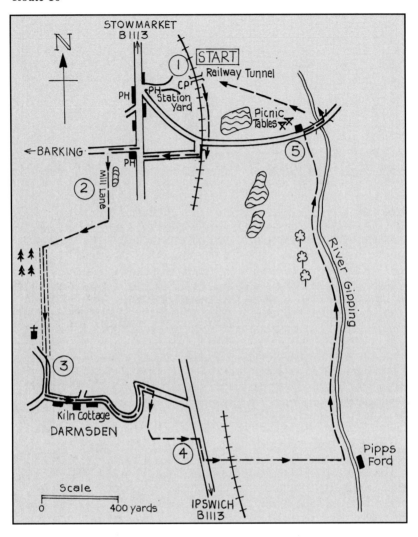

N

STOWMARKET
B1113

START
Railway Tunnel

①

CP
PH

PH
Station
Yard

Picnic
Tables

⑤

←BARKING·

PH

Mill Lane

②

River Gipping

③

Kiln Cottage
DARMSDEN

④

Pipps
Ford

Scale
0        400 yards

IPSWICH
B1113

# Route 10

## Needham Market and the Gipping Valley        5 miles

### Start

*Needham Market lies between Stowmarket and Ipswich on the old A45 (now the B1113). Cars can be parked in the station yard opposite the Swan Hotel or by the lake (B1078) road (GR 091549).*

### Route

1. *From the station yard go through the railway tunnel and turn right. Follow the path towards the lake and turn right at the car-park. Proceed under the railway bridge, bear left and follow the road to a junction with the B1113. Cross over and walk some 100 yards before turning left into Mill Lane.*

2. *Walk up the path passing a deep chalk pit on your left. At the top of the lane the path widens and skirts open fields. Straight ahead are power cables and Darmsden church. Keep bearing gradually right and turn left when you reach a wide farm track. The track heads down and then up with the church on your right.*

3. *Follow the metalled road straight ahead, keep left and head towards Darmsden. Ignore the left fork and continue past Kiln Cottage. Proceed along the road, which passes a farmyard and cottages. Halfway down the hill turn right onto a path which is not too well-defined. Follow headland around a wood and head for a tin hut standing beside an oak tree.*

4. *Cross the B1113, turn right, and walk 200 yards before turning left onto a path. Cross the railway line carefully and head straight for Pipps Ford. Turn left when meeting the Gipping Valley Footpath and follow the river on your right.*

5. *Where the path meets the junction with the B1078 turn right, walk 50 yards, and turn left to rejoin the riverside path. Cross over a wooden footbridge with the lake straight ahead. Bear right to the right side of the lake and walk past the wildlife area. Head across the field towards the station. The tunnel brings you back to the station yard.*

Willow and alder trees line the banks with swallows skimming the surface searching for flies. On warm summer evenings insects such as the Banded Demoiselle, a typical species of Suffolk's sluggish and muddy rivers, can be found. In adjacent meadowland kestrels hover, waiting to swoop down on unsuspecting mammals.

The beauty of the valley, however, is under threat from large-scale gravel extraction. Sand and gravel of course is needed for new homes and factories and some of the best and most accessible of it is in the Gipping Valley. The extraction in the short term will leave a blot on the local landscape. However, when extraction has been exhausted, a broad mix of trees will be planted. Elsewhere worked-out gravel pits have been flooded and stocked with fish, providing a welcome site for anglers while at the same time attracting such birds as moorhens, coots, tufted duck and Canada geese.

Bosmere Mill is just one of the many mills sited beside the river Gipping. A canal cut can clearly be seen which allowed barge traffic access to and from the mill. The tall four-storey wood-boarded building was converted into a restaurant, now closed.

### Public Transport
British Rail trains stop at Needham Market and Eastern Counties buses stop in the High Street near to the station yard.

### Refreshments
Bring your own picnic – tables available by the lakeside. An ice cream van usually stands in the lake car-park. In Needham Market there are two fish and chip shops and pubs which serve meals and bar snacks.

Darmsden Church

50

# Onehouse

### Outline
Community Centre – Onehouse church – Finborough Wood – Golf Course – Harleston church – Northfield Wood – Community Centre.

### Summary
This walk takes place in the heart of Suffolk and contains a mixture of fields, hedgerows, woodland and a golf course. The walk is physically undemanding but satisfying and can be shortened if wished at various intervals.

### Attractions
Despite being part of the UK's fastest growing region, Suffolk remains a predominantly farming county. Agriculture is still the largest user of land. During recent years intensive farming practices have changed the landscape. In particular, trees and hedgerows have been grubbed out to make way for the amalgamation of arable fields. The balance has to some extent been redressed with the planting of thousands of trees. Nonetheless the countryside remains a place of enchantment and discovery.

In the early springtime you may discover wild flowers such as cowslips and primroses. During warm summer days comes the smell of new mown hay. Later in the season the family may share in the pleasure of seeing corn being harvested or the sight of gulls following the plough in their search for earthworms.

Visitors often ask whether the village of Onehouse (pronounced Wun-nus by locals) literally contains one house. The idea may have originated from the old hall which in the 16th century apparently took on the grandeur of an ancient mansion. Its solitary position possibly gave its name to the parish. In 1578 Elizabeth I in one of her royal 'progresses' is supposed to have breakfasted under a large oak tree in the grounds of Onehouse Hall. Parts of the original hall, which stands near the church, still remain.

As you pass the fishing lake and start walking downhill towards the bottom of the valley, notice the thick hedgerows. Here they have been retained and provide much-needed cover for small mammals as well as nesting sites and berried larders for songbirds.

After passing through part of Finborough Wood you may care to linger awhile on the bridge which passes over the River Rat. Nowadays the river is of no commercial consequence and is often quite sluggish in appearance. However, history affirms that Caen stone used in rebuilding the abbey church at Bury St. Edmunds in the 11th century had been brought up the river to Rattlesden and then transported overland to the site.

Beyond the bridge is Finborough Park, home of Stowmarket Golf Club. Be warned, don't venture into the park or you could be hit by a flying golf ball! Later

*continued on page 54*

## Route 11

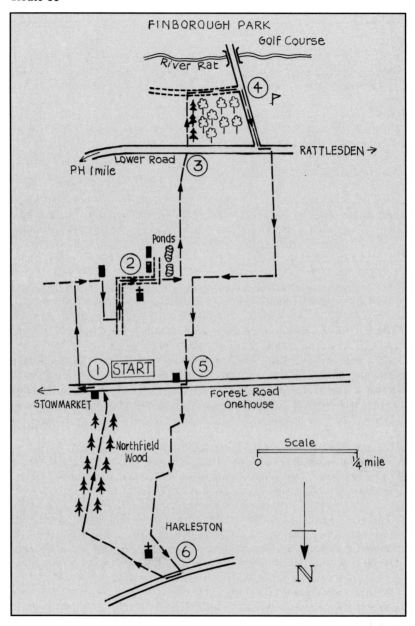

# Route 11

**Onehouse** **5 miles**

## Start

*Onehouse lies on an unmarked road west of the B1115 some 2 miles from Stowmarket. Follow the signposts to Onehouse village and park at the community centre in Forest Road (GR 020597).*

## Route

1. *From the community centre turn left down the road for 30 yards, turn right, climb over a stile and follow a path beside a hedge. At the top of the field turn right onto a farm track and walk for 40 yards before turning right again. Continue for 100 yards before bearing left onto a gravel track.*

2. *Follow the gravel track past the church, then leave it at a left-hand bend and keep straight on along a grassy track. Where it meets a field edge, turn sharp left. Keep on, with a fishing lake on the left. Cross a stile, walk downhill meet a metalled road.*

3. *Climb over a stile, cross the road and climb over another stile opposite. Walk down the path beside the wood to a wide track. Turn right along this. Keep on the track to reach a road, then turn right along this. (At this point a short detour left may be made to the river bridge and park entrance.)*

4. *Walk up the road beside the golf course and pass through iron gates at the top. Turn left and walk up the road for 10 yards before turning right onto a field path with a ditch on the right. Continue straight on for about $\frac{1}{4}$ mile and turn right into another field just after passing a wooden electricity pole. Keep beside the field headland and eventually turn left onto a path with a wide ditch on the left. At the top of the field swing right and walk beside a stagnant pond. Continue to follow the path to its junction with Forest Road.*

5. *Turn right into Forest Road, walk 20 yards, turn left and cross a ditch into the field. Follow the path and eventually pass a high laurel hedge. Swing right and left and follow the hedge. Cross a ditch into a meadow. Walk alongside the meadow and cross a rickety bridge into another meadow, Harleston church appears on the right.*

6. *Make for a stile beside a hedge at the end of the church path. Climb over the stile, turn right and walk on the road for 20 yards before turning right onto a wide track between two open fields. Keep following the track and Northfield Wood will appear on the right-hand side. Turn right onto the path which will lead to the entrance to the wood. Once in the wood, follow a wide ride. Keep going straight and continue across a footpath. Bear right when meeting a path coming from the left. From now on the path twists and turns but Forest Road will eventually appear ahead. At the road junction turn left and the car-park is right beside you.*

53

the route passes close to the second hole. Watch for the look of dismay or delight on the golfer's face as a delicate putt finds the hole or ends up in the bunker.

Further ahead the walk passes the small church at Harleston with its thatched roof. It is only recently that this ancient church joined the 20th century by installing electricity for lighting and heating.

Northfield Wood almost brings this interesting walk to a close. This is an ancient wood extensively planted with conifers which are gradually being replaced by broadleaved trees. Here children can play hide and seek in and around the wide rides.

**Public Transport**
Eastern Counties buses (infrequent service) pass by the community centre.

**Refreshments**
Shepherd and Dog public house in Lower Road.

Thatch-roofed church, Harleston

54

# Lavenham

## Outline
Churchyard – Potland Lane – Bridge Street Road – Railway Line – Park Road – Lavenham Hall – Churchyard.

## Summary
The finest medieval town in England, that's how the brochures describe Lavenham. Visitors come from all over the world to view its grand church and some of the 300 or so listed timber-framed houses and cottages. Guides listing details of historic streets and buildings are well documented elsewhere. This walk instead takes a different view of Lavenham, concentrating more on the surrounding landscape and natural habitat which includes wayside fields, hedgerows, and meadow pastures. The route of a disused railway line in particular provides a peaceful alternative to the throngs of summer tourists who visit the town.

## Attractions
Lavenham's prosperity was founded on the medieval woollen cloth industry. The local Spring family in particular acquired immense wealth and became benefactors in the building of the magnificent parish church. Thomas Spring III, known as 'The Rich Clothier' is recorded as giving £200 to 'fynysshng of the stepull'. The huge 141-feet high tower standing on a hill dominates the countryside and is clearly visible for most of the walk.

Walking along a disused railway track such as the former Great Eastern Railway branch line, brings back memories of its earlier usage. It's not difficult to close your eyes and imagine the sound of a distant whistle followed by the huffing and puffing of a small steam train making its way across the countryside. The line, which opened in 1865, finally closed to passenger trains in 1961 and for freight traffic in 1965. Lavenham station is now part of a light industrial factory site.

Closure of the line has left a rich legacy for walkers and nature lovers. The overgrown banks, trees and shrubs provide a haven for small mammals and insects. Ash, hawthorn, blackthorn and plants such as scabious and vetch grow here. The area has also proved attractive to birds like the thrush, blackbird and members of the finch family. In late summer meadowland thistles attract tortoiseshell and red admiral butterflies as well as resplendent looking goldfinches actively searching for thistle seeds.

Standing in a field beside Park Road is a concrete Pill Box. Strong Posts – the official name for such structures – were built between 1940 and 1942 mostly to defend the coast, airfields and certain key roads. This particular one like many others, would have been manned during the threat of invasion.

The remains of a tower mill standing on a mound near the Bury road are a

*continued on page 58*

55

## Route 12

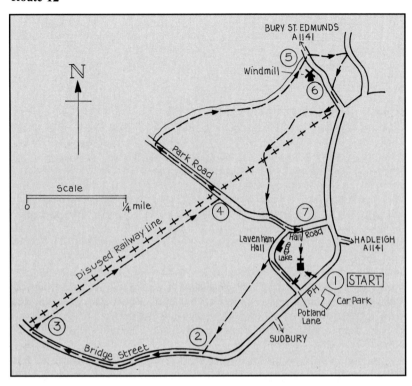

Long-tailed tit

## Route 12

### Lavenham

$3\frac{1}{2}$ **miles**

### Start

*Lavenham situated on the A1141 about 10 miles south of Bury St Edmunds. It is also signposted from the B1115. A free car-park is situated almost opposite the parish church (GR 913496).*

### Route

1. *Head out of the car-park, turn left, cross over the road and enter the churchyard. Make for Potland Lane which is situated on the left side of the church. Descend steps and bear right. Head straight on and find a path on the left that runs through a paddock. Continue along a path across an open field.*

2. *On reaching Bridge Street turn right and continue for half a mile until you reach the bridge over the disused railway line. Cross the bridge, turn left and descend into a cutting and then onto the track of the former railway.*

3. *Turn left along the track and continue until you reach the junction with Park Road.*

4. *Turn left at Park Road and walk uphill. At the top join the headland path on right. Continue walking beside the hedge and ditch until you arrive at Bury Road (A1141).*

5. *Cross over Bury Road with care and proceed up a drive onto a narrow tree-lined path. At the junction with the lane double back to the right through a paddock before reaching Bury Road again. Turn left and walk downhill. (At this spot you can keep walking ahead and eventually arrive in the High Street.)*

6. *Find a stile on the right side of the road, climb over and follow a path to a field edge. Climb over another stile and cross the railway track. After walking through meadowland you finally reach a lane. Bear left here and left again into Hall Road.*

7. *Take the path on the right beside a brick wall. Cross the stream and a grassy field with the lake and Lavenham Hall on your right. Pass through the gate and into the churchyard. The car-park is straight ahead.*

### Public Transport

Norfolk's Coaches run from Bury St Edmunds, Sudbury and Hadleigh. Chamber's Coaches run from Bury St Edmunds and Sudbury.

### Refreshments

There are various public houses and tea rooms in and around the High Street area.

reminder of the days when nearly every parish had its own mill for grinding corn. This particular structure, built in 1831 by Thomas Bear, worked until 1920 when it was pulled down. The lake close to the path at Lavenham Hall was formerly a medieval fish pond and nowadays is home to a variety of ducks and geese.

Once back at the car-park it's only a short walk to the market cross, Guildhall and other places of interest.

Lavenham

# Long Melford

**Outline**
Village Green – High Street – Hare Drift – Kentwell Hall – Holy Trinity Church – Village Green.

**Summary**
This walk starts on a large green laid out beside what is reckoned to be the longest village street in England. Take care walking beside and crossing the busy High Street.
    Hare Drift is unusual for a public bridleway in that it has a concrete surface, making it ideal for any family with a pushchair. In fact, with assistance over a couple of stiles, a pushchair can be used for most of the walk. The route takes in views of Kentwell Hall standing at the head of a mile of pollarded lime trees. Before the walk ends the path diverts from the avenue and gives the opportunity to look around the exterior of the magnificent Holy Trinity Church.

**Attractions**
Arguably the best time to walk along Hare Drift is in the springtime when birdsong and the greenery of the tall hedgerows and woodland are at their best. The route passes near to the much-needed bypass road, but the noise from passing vehicles is only temporary, the walk soon switches to fields and meadowland where children can run ahead and cross over stiles at will.
    Kentwell Hall is a superb Elizabethan manor house. A walk to view the house beyond its wrought iron gates is highly recommended. Entrance fees are charged for admittance to the house and gardens and also to the farm. 'Kentwell 1578' comes alive each year, usually mid-June to mid-July, when the manor prepares to receive Queen Elizabeth II. Tudor domestic life is re-enacted using Tudor artifacts, clothes and speech. No doubt the catering is well-organised these days. Four centuries ago however, a dissatisfied Elizabeth I is said to have dubbed the stately home, 'Hungry Hall'.
    During autumn parties of the tit and finch families flit through the Hall's avenue of pollarded lime trees looking for seeds. Cattle and sheep can often be seen grazing on nearby pastureland.
    Long Melford, like many other south Suffolk villages, gained its wealth from the wool industry. After the demise of the local cloth trade, the craft of weaving survived and at different periods the village witnessed the establishment of silk, horsehair and coconut matting industries.
    The celebrated church of The Holy Trinity standing at the top of the green was built between 1460 and 1495 by members of the Clopton family and other wealthy local wool merchants. Situated on the edge of the churchyard is the intricate red-brick Holy Trinity Hospital (almshouses) founded in 1573 and remodelled in 1847.

*continued on page 62*

**Route 13**

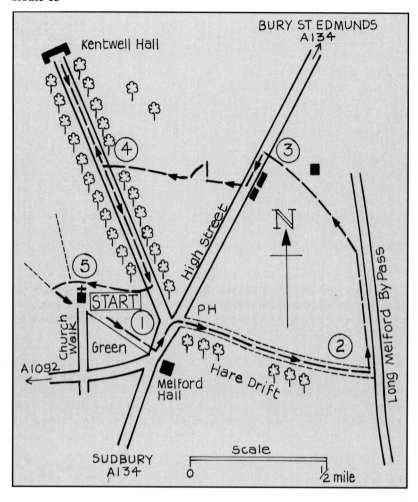

Kentwell Hall

BURY ST EDMUNDS
A134

High Street

③

N

④

⑤

START

①

PH

Church Walk

Green

②

Long Melford By Pass

A1092

Melford Hall

Hare Drift

scale

SUDBURY
A134

0                    ½ mile

60

# Route 13

## Long Melford $2\frac{1}{2}$ miles

### Start

*Long Melford lies between Bury St Edmunds and Sudbury on the A134 road, 15 miles from Bury St Edmunds and 3 miles from Sudbury. Parking on or near the Green (GR 866468).*

### Route

1. *Cross the Green, turn left into High Street and cross the road. Almost opposite the entrance to Kentwell Hall is a public bridleway named Hare Drift. Follow the bridleway past the garden centre to reach the Long Melford Bypass after about $\frac{3}{4}$ mile. Continue walking straight ahead.*

2. *Immediately before the bridleway meets the bypass, turn left along a footpath. The path eventually bears to the left. Walk around the side of a wide metal gate and continue on a gravel track. With a farm machinery depot on the right, turn left and cross into a field entrance.*

3. *Follow the path until you reach the A134. Turn left, walk for 50 yards, cross the road and take the path on the right. Follow it for 100 yards, bear right and find a stile on the left. Cross over the stile and head for the opposite side of the meadow to reach the avenue leading to Kentwell Hall.*

4. *Cross over a stile and turn right. Walk up the avenue for extensive views of Kentwell Hall. Turn around and return down the avenue. Just before the avenue ends look for a path on the righthand side.*

5. *Keep on the path and, when you meet another path, turn left. After a short distance bear left again. Find the road at the rear of the church and return to the Green.*

### Public Transport

Bus services to the village are operated by Theobalds Coaches, Chambers Buses and Rules Coaches. Nearest BR station is Sudbury 3 miles away.

### Refreshments

There are tea shops and public houses in the centre of the village.
Kentwell Hall: For details of opening times and special events Tel. 0787 310207.

In days past the large triangular green of 14 acres was used for horse fairs and as a yearly market for cattle. Nowadays the green can be enjoyed for picnicking and for children to play ball or run around.

Standing almost opposite the green and across the road is Long Melford's other Tudor mansion, Melford Hall, now National Trust property and open to the public.

Kentwell Hall

# Ickworth Park

## Outline
Car-park – Canal Walk – Fairy Lake – Lady Katherine's Wood – Lownde Wood – Deer Enclosure – Car-park.

## Summary
The Ickworth estate came into the hands of the Hervey family in the 15th century but nowadays ownership of the house, park and estate has passed to the National Trust. The latter incidentally charges a fee for entry into the park which goes towards the upkeep of the paths. Although it's possible to walk eleven miles around the park boundaries, this walk has been shortened to about five and a half miles. The waymarked route passes through undulating countryside which includes lakes, parkland and ancient woodland. Although younger children may not want to venture too far along the route, their patience will be rewarded with a visit to the deer enclosure. Also a play area for children of all ages may prove inviting.

## Attractions
Spacious surroundings, sheep quietly grazing and an extraordinary oval house are just some of the varied sights that greet you as you enter the park and make your way up a long avenue towards the car-park.

Ickworth House (open to the public) with its domed, elliptical rotunda was the idea of Frederick Augustus Hervey, the 4th Earl of Derry who intended that his mansion would display works of art collected on his European tours. Sadly the collection, worth an estimated £20,000 at the time, was confiscated by the French army in 1798. The Earl died before his mansion was completed and it was left to his son, the 1st Marquis of Bristol, to finish his father's eccentric scheme.

As you begin the walk you will soon be aware of the various mature trees which grace the park. Most are pollarded oaks but there are also hornbeam, beech and field maple. The famous landscape gardener 'Capability' Brown is thought to have contributed to the general layout of the park which nowadays is recognised for the importance of its specimen trees. Apart from the rotunda building there are other reminders of the Hervey family to be seen on the walk. St. Michael's church (not open to the public) is where past generations of the family have been married and buried. On the southern boundary of the park is an obelisk some 50 feet tall. It was built to the memory of the Earl-Bishop by the people of Londonderry in 1817.

The route offers a number of delights and surprises. None more so perhaps than the almost unexpected appearance of the Fairy Lake, a favourite haunt of great crested grebes, tufted duck, coot and moorhens. A little further on in Lady Katherine's Wood is a partially secluded roundhouse.

From a raised platform hide, red and fallow deer can be watched unobtrusively. A visit to the children's play area near the car-park may prove worthwhile as might a picnic eaten in spacious surroundings of the Park.

## Route 14

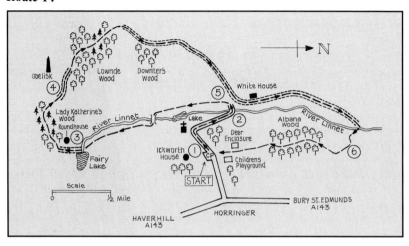

Goldcrest

## Route 14

**Ickworth Park**                                   **$5\frac{1}{2}$ miles or 3 miles**

**Start**

*Ickworth Park is located in Horringer village, 3 miles SW of Bury St Edmunds on the A143 (GR 826620).*

**Route**

1. *From the car-park proceed to the Park driveway and continue downhill passing St Michael's church on the left.*

2. *Continue downhill and after crossing the River Linnet, turn left and walk beside it. Pass through an area of scrub and hedge. Cross over a footbridge and follow the path through a large spinney and arrive at the Fairy Lake.*

3. *Turn right and walk uphill through Lady Katherine's Wood, keeping the roundhouse on the right. The path now joins a flinty track. At laurel bushes turn right and walk through a wooded area. At the top turn right onto a wide track.*

4. *Continue on the track which skirts Lownde Wood. The obelisk will shortly appear on the left. The path now enters Lownde Wood. Continue walking past tall oak trees and at the exit to the wood cross over a ditch and turn right onto a flint drive. Proceed downhill for about a mile, passing Downter's Wood on the way.*

5. *At the bottom of the hill you can walk straight ahead, cross the bridge over the River Linnet and walk back to the car-park. Alternatively turn left onto a sandy track and walk beside the River Linnet for 1 mile to a wooden bridge. Turn right and proceed up and down steps to cross the river. Turn left and follow a path around a field headland for 400 yards.*

6. *Bear left and walk uphill through Albana Wood. The deer enclosure will eventually appear on your right. Continue back to the car-park.*

**Public Transport**

Eastern Counties service to Haverhill passes the park entrance in Horringer village.

**Refreshments**

A restaurant and shop are located in the Rotunda building. The Park is open daily 7 am–7 pm.

Ickworth House

Lake, West Stow

66

# West Stow

## Outline

Car-park – Visitor Centre – Anglo Saxon Village – Lakeside – River Lark – Bird Hide – Car-park.

## Summary

This undemanding walk more or less follows the inside perimeter of the 125-acre country park at West Stow. The walk circles a large lake formerly a gravel pit, passes through woodland and follows a stretch of the River Lark. Optional visits can be made to a bird-hide and to an informative visitor centre. For the price of an admission fee, you can also visit a reconstructed Anglo Saxon village. Additionally for children there is a nature trail and comprehensive play area.

## Attractions

The light sandy soil and open heathland around West Stow is typical of that to be found in an area known as Breckland. It takes its name from the natural area of the 'Brecks' (areas of heathland periodically cultivated). Here you are following in the footsteps of Neolithic man, and the Saxons and Romans who frequented these parts. Icknield Way, claimed to be the oldest road in England, passes by just outside the park boundary.

Where huge amounts of gravel have been extracted, the resulting pits have been flooded to form a new lake. This in turn has provided a welcome haven for wildfowl which nest on the man-made islands. Birds seen on the water include flocks of Canada geese, great crested and little grebe as well as coot and moorhen. If you are lucky you may see a motionless heron patiently waiting to pounce on an unsuspecting fish.

The southern side of the park is bounded by the River Lark. Horse-drawn barges used to pass by here with cargoes of coal for delivery to Bury St Edmunds. Beyond the remains of a river lock a bird-hide looks across to a flooded gravel pit. Since the pit is some distance away, binoculars are recommended, if only to watch cormorants drying out their outstretched wings.

A visitor centre, located a short distance from the car-park, seeks to explain the history of the local breckland habitat. The centre also gives an insight into day-to-day management tasks carried out by park wardens. Information on many of the plants, trees and animals to be found in the park is highlighted on posts positioned at selected intervals around a compact nature trail. In the middle of the park is a reconstruction of an Anglo Saxon village. Primitive huts have been built on a former settlement using tools and techniques available to the Anglo Saxons. Craft demonstrations are given and enthusiasts in Anglo Saxon costume re-enact the lifestyle of the original inhabitants.

Close to the car-park is a play area. Picnic tables are close by.

# Route 15

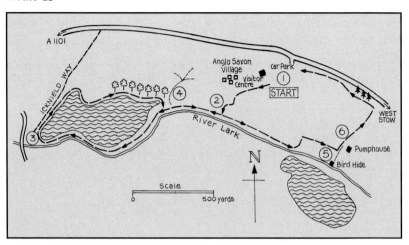

Reconstructed Anglo Saxon village

# Route 15

## West Stow                                                    2 miles

### Start
*West Stow Country Park is located off the A1101 Bury St Edmunds to Mildenhall road between the villages of West Stow and Icklingham. Entrance to car-park (GR 801715).*

### Route

1. *From the car-park make for the visitor centre (optional) and proceed along a path passing left of the reconstructed Anglo Saxon village. Pass through a small spinney and meet the river towpath.*

2. *Turn right and walk beside the river. When the lake comes into view bear left keeping between the river on your left and the lake on the right.*

3. *Keep following the path around the perimeter of the lake. Eventually the path passes through woodland but soon after meets the lakeside again.*

4. *Where the path meets the river towpath turn left. Continue to walk on the towpath until you reach the remains of a river lock. Here the path swings left to a junction with another path. Turn right along this.*

5. *Keep on the path and fork right to visit the bird hide. Otherwise, fork left and join the road beside the old pumphouse.*

6. *Continue down the road for 150 yards. The path turns left just before reaching the road that leads to West Stow village. Walk beside an area of pine trees and eventually reach the car-park.*


### Public Transport
Eastern Counties service between Bury St Edmunds and Mildenhall passes within approx 1 mile of the park. Ipswich Buses and Neals Travel operate a limited Sunday and Public Holiday service and stop outside the park entrance.


### Refreshments
A kiosk serves light refreshments during summer months. A drinks dispensing machine is located in the visitor centre.

Stud farm near Gazeley

# Gazeley, Moulton and Dalham

**Outline**
Gazeley Church – Moulton Church – Packhorse Bridge – River Kennett –
Catford Bridge – Malt Kiln – Dalham Church – Bridge Kiln Wood –
Blocksey Wood – Bluebutton Wood – Gazeley Church.

**Summary**
For a county not particularly noted for slope and variety, this walk is very
rewarding and must rate as one of the best circular walks in Suffolk. Gentle descents
and steady uphill climbs come as a pleasant surprise on a route situated near the
Cambridgeshire border. Much of the walk follows the course of the River Kennett
and offers superb scenic views of the Kennett valley and the surrounding
countryside. Excursions are made on well-defined paths through woodland and
alongside field headlands. Known locally as 'The Three Churches Walk' the walk
passes each of the churches of Gazeley, Moulton and Dalham. Motorists using the
busy A45 are probably unaware (thank goodness!) that hidden from view a mile or
two away are delightful villages and leafy lanes just waiting to be explored. Children
will find the 15th century packhorse bridge of interest and also the horses to be seen
in the paddocks of a local stud farm. For the thirsty or hungry there is a pub
conveniently sited in each village. The walk is well waymarked and can be shortened
in places by following alternative routes shown on the map.

**Attractions**
Shortly after leaving Gazeley you walk past a stud farm. Horses are very much part
of the scene around here. Newmarket, the headquarters of British horse racing, is
only 5 miles away. After walking for $\frac{3}{4}$ mile or so on a metalled road, you cross a field
and are immediately rewarded with the landscape opening up to reveal views of the
county border and the village of Moulton nestling below in the Kennett valley. On a
clear day the outline of Ely Cathedral is clearly visible away in the distant
Cambridgeshire fens.

   At Moulton you have the choice of shortening the route by walking through the
church graveyard and re-joining the path further on. However, by so doing you will
miss the ancient packhorse bridge. The four-arched bridge, nowadays maintained
by English Heritage, stands on an old route from Cambridge to Bury St Edmunds.

   In a dry season the river Kennett is no more than a rivulet here. But do not be
deceived. Nearby marker poles, somewhat optimistically perhaps, suggest that in
the event of flooding, water could rise anything up to three feet. Occasionally after a
period of prolonged rainfall flooding does indeed occur. Photographs hanging in
the bar at the Affleck Arms in Dalham show the whole village awash.

   As you pass Moulton church look up and spot the fish on the weather vane. Very

*continued on page 74*

71

# Route 16

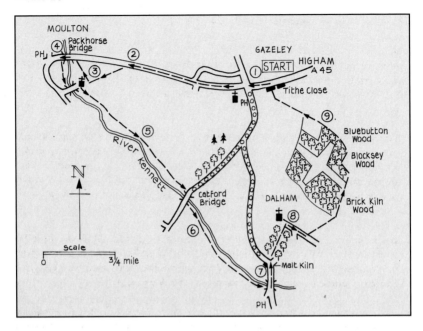

## Gazeley, Moulton and Dalham

$6\frac{1}{2}$ miles or $4\frac{1}{2}$ miles

### Start

*Gazeley is signposted south off the A45 between Newmarket and Bury St Edmunds. Park near the Chequers public house (GR 720642). (This walk can also be started from either Moulton or Dalham.)*

### Route

1. *Find the path starting from beside Gazeley church. The path continues alongside the graveyard before passing between paddocks of the local stud farm. The path steadily climbs and eventually meets a metalled road.*

2. *Keep straight on the road for $\frac{3}{4}$ mile. As the road starts to go down a hill, find a path on the left and pass through a field entrance. Cross the field and climb over a stile into a meadow. Walk downhill through the meadow on a well-worn path. Cross over a stile, continue on a steep path and arrive at the rear of Moulton church. (**To shorten the walk** go through the graveyard and turn left after the church along the riverside footpath.)*

# Route 16 (*continued*)

3. *The path bears right and after passing between a hedge and a meadow, it widens and changes to a concrete surface. At the end of the path turn left onto a road and make for the packhorse bridge around the corner.*

4. *Just past the bridge turn left and walk beside the river. Ignore wooden and brick-arched bridges but at the junction with Church Road, cross over the river by means of a bridge with metal railings. Turn right, walk past the church and join a bridleway which gets narrower before opening up beside a high bank with the river below.*

5. *The path continues through open fields with a high hedge on the right. Eventually the river re-appears again. Follow a path past a sewage works and reach a junction with the road. At the junction turn right, walk 50 yards, crossing over Catford Bridge, and turn sharp left through a field entrance to re-join the path with the river now on the left. For a short-cut back to Gazeley turn left at the bridge and follow the road back into the village.*

6. *Keep following the path and ignore any field entrances on the left. Soon the outline of the mill at Dalham will appear on the right-hand skyline. Shortly after the path bears to the left, a stile will appear. Cross over the stile and walk beside a small paddock, turn left and cross the river by a white footbridge.*

7. *Turn left, walk up a metalled road and pass the malt kiln. Turn right through a wooden kissing gate. Follow the path uphill to the church, then pass through a metal kissing gate and turn right onto the road.*

8. *The road goes downhill and then up. Ignore a road turning to the right. The path goes sharp left through a wooded area and follows a field headland before entering Brick Kiln Wood. The path continues along the edge of the wood and shortly arrives at a clearing. Keep on the well-waymarked path as it enters and passes through Blocksey and Bluebutton Woods.*

9. *After leaving Bluebutton Wood the path gets narrower and passes a plantation of young trees before opening out beside a field headland. Keep walking straight ahead and follow wooden electricity poles beside a grassy track. Walk down the track with Gazeley church appearing in the distance. The path finally crosses an arable field and enters a housing estate (Tithe Close). Walk down Higham Road and return to the starting point.*

appropriate since the patron saint is St Peter. As the walk progresses you will discover a variety of bridges crossing the river. Some are brick-arched while others are made of metal and wood. Walking along the bridleway you may encounter riders exercising their horses. Here the riverbanks are quite high and overlook the Kennett which disappears and returns from time to time.

In the village of Dalham have a look at the delightful thatched cottages and neat gardens. Also worthy of note is the unusual conical malt kiln. The nearby address of Maltings Farm suggests perhaps that it was the site of locally-produced malt before the industry finally became modernised. A real highlight of the walk is the steady climb to Dalham church through a beautiful avenue of chestnut trees. The 650-year-old church stands in the grounds of Dalham Hall where the family of Cecil Rhodes, founder of Rhodesia, once lived. In 1625 the church tower collapsed and was rebuilt in 1627. Today it's without its spire which, like Oliver Cromwell, came to a sudden end on 3 September 1658.

Much of the remaining walk passes through lonely stretches of woodland. In early springtime much of the woodland floor is carpeted with wild flowers. The trees are a mixture of broad leaved and conifer. When foliage becomes dense woodland birds become harder to spot and are frequently heard rather than seen. Though initially the path may seem to lose direction as it passes through the woods, inexperienced walkers may be reassured that the route is well waymarked throughout.


**Public Transport**
Cambus and Eastern Counties run from Newmarket and Bury St Edmunds.


**Refreshments**
Public Houses: Gazeley – The Chequers. Moulton – Kings Head. Dalham – Affleck Arms.

Common spotted orchid

# Useful Information

## Routes in Order of Difficulty

Few of the following routes could be considered difficult in terms of physical effort. However before starting, as these are Family Walks, some thought should be given to the length of each walk, especially where younger children are concerned.

Starting with the easiest:

Route  7  Christchurch Park (1½ miles)
Route  6  Pipers Vale (2 miles)
Route  9  Hadleigh (2 miles)
Route  3  Iken & River Alde (3 miles)
Route 13  Long Melford (2½ miles)
Route  4  Waldringfield (2½ miles)
Route 15  West Stow (2 miles)
Route  2  Framlingham (2 miles)
Route  1  Dunwich (3½ miles)
Route 11  Onehouse (5 miles)
Route 12  Lavenham (3½ miles)
Route 14  Ickworth Park (5½ miles)
Route  8  Flatford & Constable Country (4 miles)
Route 10  Needham Market & Gipping Valley (5 miles)
Route  5  Trimley St Mary (5 miles)
Route 16  Gazeley, Moulton & Dalham (6½ miles)

## Wet Weather Alternatives
Completely or partly under cover.

### Museums and Art Galleries

**Aldeburgh**  Moot Hall, Sea Front. Town history and maritime affairs. Tel 0728 452158.

**Bury St Edmunds**  Moyse's Hall Museum, Cornhill. Local archaeology, natural history, guns, toys, costume and porcelain. Tel 0284 757072 (weekends 756043)

**Bury St Edmunds**  Art Gallery, Cornhill. Market Cross building re-clad by Robert Adams. Former playhouse. Contemporary art exhibitions. Tel 0248 762081.

**Dunwich Museum**  St James' Street. History of Dunwich from Roman times, chronicling its disappearance into the sea over the centuries. Local natural history. Tel 072 873358.

**Felixstowe**  Landguard Fort and Museum. Maps, documents, photographs, and artefacts illustrating history of the 18c. fort. Tel 0394 286403.

**Ipswich**  Museum and Exhibition Gallery, High Street. Natural history, geology, archaeology and ethnography. Collection of British birds. Tel 0473 213761.

**Leiston**  Long Shop Museum, Main Street. Award-winning steam and industrial museum. Tel 0729 832189/830550.

**Newmarket**  Horse Racing Museum, High Street. History of British Horce Racing over 300 years, housed in Regency subscription rooms. Tel 0638 667333.

**Orford**  Dunwich Underwater Exploration Exhibition, The Craft Shop, Front Street. Marine archaeology and artefacts. Tel 0394 450678.

**Stowmarket**  Museum of East Anglian Life, Iliffe Way. Collection of East Anglia's rural past. Craft workshops and demonstrations. Tel 0449 612229.

76

## Castles and Historic Houses

**Framlingham Castle** Built in 12th century by the Bigod family (Earls of Norfolk). One of the finest examples of a curtain-walled castle. Tel 0728 724189.

**Ickworth House** Horringer Village. National Trust. Rotunda building, park and gardens. Tel 0284 735270.

**Lavenham** Guildhall. History of the wool and cloth industries. Also, artefacts relating to historic Lavenham. Tel 0787 247646.

**Long Melford** Melford Hall. Tudor mansion and gardens. Tel 0787 880286.

**Long Melford** Kentwell Hall. Elizabethan manor house with moat and gardens. Stages historical re-creation of events. Tel 0787 310207.

## Leisure Centres and Swimming Pools

| | |
|---|---|
| Crown Swimming Pools, Ipswich | Tel 0473 255007 |
| Felixstowe Leisure Centre | Tel 0394 670411 |
| Gainsborough Leisure Centre, Ipswich | Tel 0473 716900 |
| Hadleigh Swimming Pool | Tel 0473 823470 |
| Mid Suffolk Leisure Centre, Stowmarket | Tel 0449 674980 |

Old pumphouse, West Stow (route 15)

77

## Other Places of Interest

**Easton Farm Park** Wickham Market. Victorian model farm. Farm animals, nature trail and demonstrations of milking etc. Tel 0728 746475.

**Framlingham** Shawsgate Vineyard, Badingham Road. Guided tours of winery and tastings. Tel 0728 724060.

**Snape Maltings** Boat trips on River Alde. Shops and galleries. Tel 072 888303.

**Waldringfield** Boat trips on River Deben. Tel 0473 36260. Working dairy farm. Tel 0284 728862.

**West Stow** Meadows Farm.

Note: It is important to check opening times with either the attraction itself or the nearest Tourist Information Office since such times are often subject to change.

## Public Transport

For details of operators and timetables contact the following:

| | |
|---|---|
| Cambus (Cambridge) | Tel 0223 423554 |
| Chambers Buses (Bures) | Tel 0787 227233 |
| Eastern Counties (Ipswich) | Tel 0473 253734 |
| Eastern Counties (Bury St Edmunds) | Tel 0284 766171 |
| Neals Coaches (Newmarket) | Tel 0638 720302 |
| Norfolks Coaches (Nayland) | Tel 0206 262925 |
| Partridge Coaches (Hadleigh) | Tel 0473 822314 |
| Rules Coaches (Boxford) | Tel 0206 210260 |
| British Rail (Ipswich) | Tel 0473 690744 |

## Tourist Information Offices

| | |
|---|---|
| Bury St Edmunds, Angel Hill | Tel 0284 764667 |
| Felixstowe, Leisure Centre | Tel 0394 670411 |
| Hadleigh, Toppersfield Hall | Tel 0473 822922 |
| Ipswich, Town Hall | Tel 0473 258070 |
| Lavenham, Guildhall | Tel 0787 248207 |
| Stowmarket, Wilkes Way | Tel 0449 676800 |

Packhorse Bridge (route 16)

Clare, near Long Melford (route 13)

## THE FAMILY WALKS SERIES

**Family Walks on Anglesey.** Laurence Main. ISBN 0 907758 665.

**Family Walks in Berkshire & North Hampshire.** Kathy Sharp. ISBN 0 907758 371.

**Family Walks around Bristol, Bath & the Mendips.** Nigel Vile. ISBN 0 907758 193.

**Family Walks around Cardiff & the Valleys.** Gordon Hindess. ISBN 0 907758 541.

**Family Walks in Cheshire.** Chris Buckland. ISBN 0 907758 290.

**Family Walks in Cornwall.** John Caswell. ISBN 0 907758 55X.

**Family Walks in the Cotswolds.** Gordon Ottewell. ISBN 0 907758 150.

**Family Walks on Exmoor & the Quantocks.** John Caswell. ISBN 0 907758 460.

**Family Walks in South Gloucestershire.** Gordon Ottewell. ISBN 0 907758 339.

**Family Walks in Gower.** Amanda Green. ISBN 0 907758 630.

**Family Walks in Hereford and Worcester.** Gordon Ottewell. ISBN 0 907758 207.

**Family Walks on the Isle of Wight.** Laurence Main. ISBN 0 907758 568.

**Family Walks in North West Kent.** Clive Cutter. ISBN 0 907758 363.

**Family Walks in the Lake District.** Barry McKay. ISBN 0 907758 401.

**Family Walks in Mendip, Avalon & Sedgemoor.** Nigel Vile. ISBN 0 907758 41X.

**Family Walks in the New Forest.** Nigel Vile. ISBN 0 907758 606.

**Family Walks in Oxfordshire.** Laurence Main. ISBN 0 907758 38X.

**Family Walks in the Dark Peak.** Norman Taylor. ISBN 0 907758 169.

**Family Walks in the White Peak.** Norman Taylor. ISBN 0 907758 096.

**Family Walks in South Derbyshire.** Gordon Ottewell. ISBN 0 907758 614.

**Family Walks in South Shropshire.** Marian Newton. ISBN 0 907758 304.

**Family Walks in Snowdonia.** Laurence Main. ISBN 0 907758 320.

**Family Walks in the Staffordshire Peaks and Potteries.** Les Lumsdon. ISBN 0 907758 347.

**Family Walks around Stratford & Banbury.** Gordon Ottewell. ISBN 0 907758 495.

**Family Walks in Suffolk.** C J Francis. ISBN 0 907758 649.

**Family Walks around Swansea.** Raymond Humphreys. ISBN 0 907758 622.

**Family Walks in the Teme Valley.** Camilla Harrison. ISBN 0 907758 452.

**Family Walks in Three Peaks & Malham.** Howard Beck. ISBN 0 907758 428

**Family Walks in Mid Wales.** Laurence Main. ISBN 0 907758 274.

**Family Walks in the North Wales Borderlands.** Gordon Emery. ISBN 0 907758 509.

**Family Walks in Warwickshire.** Geoff Allen. ISBN 0 907758 533.

**Family Walks in the Weald of Kent & Sussex.** Clive Cutter. ISBN 0 907758 517.

**Family Walks in Wiltshire.** Nigel Vile. ISBN 0 907758 215.

**Family Walks in the Wye Valley.** Heather & Jon Hurley. ISBN 0 907758 266.

**Family Walks in the North Yorkshire Dales.** Howard Beck. ISBN 0 907758 525.

**Family Walks in South Yorkshire.** Norman Taylor. ISBN 0 907758 258.

**Family Walks in West Yorkshire.** Howard Beck. ISBN 0 907758 436.

*The publishers welcome suggestions for further titles in this series; and will be pleased to consider manuscripts relating to Derbyshire from new or established authors.*

Scarthin Books of Cromford, in the Peak District, are also leading second-hand and antiquarian booksellers, and are eager to purchase specialised material, both ancient and modern.

Contact Dr D. J. Mitchell, 0629-823272.